U0065808

喜捨篇
智慧法語

放下、服務、奉獻

心道

The way of Mind II :
Words of wisdom

第二輯

Joyful Giving:
Letting Go
and Serving Others

心道法師 語錄
By Dharma
Master Hsin Tao

# 目錄

# Contents

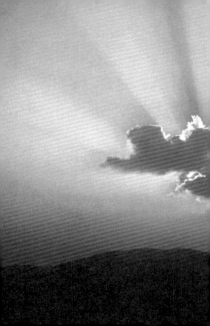

作者簡介

The Way of Mind II : Words of wisdom

　　心道法師一九四八年生，祖籍雲南，幼失依怙，為滇緬邊境孤雛。十三歲隨孤軍撤移來台，十五歲初聞觀音菩薩聖號，有感於觀音菩薩的悲願，以「悟性報觀音」、「吾不成佛誓不休」、「真如度眾生」刺身供佛，立誓

6

智慧法語

喜捨篇

Joyful Giving:
Letting Go
and Serving Others

放下、服務、奉獻

徹悟真理，救度苦難。

　　二十五歲出家後，頭陀行腳歷十餘年，前後在台北外雙溪、宜蘭礁溪圓明寺、莿仔崙墳塔、龍潭公墓和員山周舉人廢墟，體驗世間最幽隱不堪的「塚間修」，矢志修證，了脫生死，覺悟本來。

Joyful Giving:
Letting Go
and Serving Others

喜捨篇
智慧法語

放下、服務、奉獻

生道場」，展開弘法度
生的佛行事業，為現代
人擘劃成佛地圖。為了
推動宗教共存共榮，法
師以慈悲的華嚴理念奔
走國際，並於二〇〇一
年十一月成立世界宗教
博物館，致力於各種不
同宗教的對話，提昇對
所有宗教的寬容、尊重

滿足。這些年來，心道法師以禪的攝心觀照為本、教育弘法為主軸，用慈悲願力守護人類心靈，以世界和平為終生職志，帶領大眾實踐利益眾生的宏大願力，祈願佛陀法脈永傳不息，讓佛法真諦普傳後世。

Brief Introduction to the Author

Born in upper Myanmar in 1948 to ethnic Chinese parents of Yunnan Province, Master Hsin Tao was left orphaned and impoverished at an early age. Having been taken in by the remnants of

Joyful Giving:
Letting Go
and Serving Others

喜捨篇

智慧法語

放下、服務、奉獻

ROC military units operating along the border of Yunnan, China, he was brought to Taiwan in 1961 when he was 13. At the age of 15, he was deeply moved by the compassion of Guanyin Bodhisattva

Joyful Giving:
Letting Go
and Serving Others

喜捨篇

智慧法語

放下、服務、奉獻

of Guanyin," "I will never rest until Buddhahood is attained," and "Liberating all beings by living in Suchness."

After becoming a Buddhist monk at the age of 25 and making

a vow to attain
enlightenment, Master
Hsin Tao traveled on
foot for over ten years,
practicing austerities
in lonely and secluded
locations, including
Waishuangxi in
Taipei, Yuanming
Temple in Yilan,

Chingtzulun Grave
Tower, Longtan
Cemetery, and the
ruins of the first-
degree Scholar Chou
in Yuanshan, Yilan
county.

Having arrived at
the Fahua Cave on
Fulong Mountain in

early 1983, Master
Hsin Tao undertook
a fast which was to
last over two years,
during which time he
attained deep insight
into the meaning
of "Only when all
beings are liberated,
is enlightenment fully

Joyful Giving:
Letting Go
and Serving Others

喜捨篇
智慧法語

放下、服務、奉獻

attained." Standing on the summit of the Ling Jiou Mountain, looking down at the Pacific Ocean, Master Hsin Tao felt great compassion for the suffering of all sentient beings. After his solitary retreat

In addition, Master Hsin Tao strived hard to gain international support with the compassionate spirit of the Buddhist Avatamsaka Vision (of the interconnectedness of all beings in the universe), and

Joyful Giving:
Letting Go
and Serving Others

喜捨篇

智慧法語

放下、服務、奉獻

of world peace and a promoting awareness of our global family for love and peace through interreligious dialogues. The spirit of MWR is enshrined in the words "Respect, Tolerance, and Love."

The ideal of Chan

lives through the spirit of "Prajñā" or Enlightened Wisdom. And he hopes for them to practice Buddha's teachings unceasingly, and learn to stop clinging, so that tranquility and contentment of mind

Through compassion, he makes great efforts to protect and care for all sentient beings. Taking the establishment of world peace as his lifelong commitment, he leads people to work for the great cause of

心之道 智慧法語（第二輯）
**喜捨篇**-放下、服務、奉獻

The Way of Mind II:
Words of wisdom
**Joyful Giving :**
Letting Go and Serving Others

懂得喜捨、懂得為善，
人間就是淨土。

Joyful Giving:
Letting Go
and Serving Others

喜捨篇
智慧法語

放下、服務、奉獻

When we understand
joyful giving, we act in
a wholesome manner
and create a pure land in
the here and now.

不要執著於眼前
這個日子的好好壞壞，
要為未來的好緣
做無盡的布施。

Joyful Giving:
Letting Go
and Serving Others

喜捨篇
智慧法語

放下、服務、奉獻

Rather than dwelling
on what's good or
bad about the present,
it would be better to
create the conditions
for a brighter future by
practicing generosity
as much as possible.

Refraining from
bickering is positive,
not negative.

人最可愛的地方
就是誠懇，
誠懇是最好的公關。

Joyful Giving:
Letting Go
and Serving Others

喜捨篇
智慧法語

放下、服務、奉獻

Sincerity is a form of
beauty; it also makes
for highly effective
public relations.

喜歡付出而不要求，
才能擁有無負擔的快樂

Giving without expecting
anything in return brings
unencumbered happiness.

When seen as a form
of giving, work
becomes energizing.

廣修供養，
就是常常無私地
去做布施的工作。

Regularly practicing
selfless generosity is a
way of making offerings
to the Triple Gem.

培養付出、給予、喜捨
不要培養貪、瞋、癡，
這就是廣修供養的意義

Cultivate joyful giving, not greed, hatred and delusion; this is what is meant by making offerings to the Triple Gem.

Joyful Giving:
Letting Go
and Serving Others

喜捨篇 智慧法語

放下、服務、奉獻

Awakening means opening
up and letting go.

多做福報的事，
多結善緣，
就會讓你反敗為勝。

Joyful Giving:
Letting Go
and Serving Others

喜捨篇

智慧法語

放下、服務、奉獻

Doing good and
establishing
wholesome affinities,
you can never
go wrong.

常常站在別人的立場
去想，服務、利他，
人緣就會好。

First place yourself
in another's position,
then strive to benefit
others. This way, you
always get along well
with others.

逃避不叫作「丟掉」，
因為不做它、不想它，
都是另一種錯覺。

Joyful Giving:
Letting Go
and Serving Others

放下、服務、奉獻

It's impossible to be free
of something by trying to
escape from it.

唯有覺悟到
一切因緣好壞，
都是短暫、曇花一現，
才能遠離虛幻，
定下心來。

Joyful Giving:
Letting Go
and Serving Others

喜捨篇
智慧法語

放下、服務、奉獻

Realizing that all
conditioned things,
good or bad, are
impermanent, the
mind becomes clear
and tranquil.

有緣在一起就彼此珍惜
時間若結束，也不要
牽戀，輪迴的世界
就是不斷變化的時間，
是永遠抓不住
也留不住的。

Joyful Giving:
Letting Go
and Serving Others

喜捨篇
智慧法語

放下、服務、奉獻

We remain with our loved
ones only as long as the
conditions are suitable.
Cherish your time together
without being attached,
for all things must pass.

如果不能看開、放下，
就沒有辦法前進，
只能活在過去的回憶裡

Joyful Giving:
Letting Go
and Serving Others

喜捨篇
智慧法語

放下、服務、奉獻

If we can't accept
things as they are and
let go, then we remain
stuck in the past.

不計較、不煩惱，
放下就是快樂。

Joyful Giving:
Letting Go
and Serving Others

喜捨篇
智慧法語

放下、服務、奉獻

Be done with bickering
and worry; letting go
is happiness.

留戀是一種壞習氣，
要慢慢去除，除光了，
就少有罣礙。

Joyful Giving:
Letting Go
and Serving Others

喜捨篇
智慧法語

放下、服務、奉獻

Attachment is a bad
habit; the more you
free yourself from its
clutches, the fewer
your hindrances.

Emancipate your
mind from all that
shackles it.

修行是讓
發生的一切境界過去，
每一時刻發生的事情
都在消失，
所以不要貪著。

Joyful Giving:
Letting Go
and Serving Others

喜捨篇
智慧法語

放下、服務、奉獻

Spiritual practice means
allowing all conditioned
things to come and go.
Everything that arises is
bound to pass, so there's
no point in clinging
to any of it.

為什麼生起煩惱？
因為心執著障礙，
貪瞋癡慢疑就跟著出來
所以要「捨」。

Joyful Giving:
Letting Go
and Serving Others

喜捨篇

智慧法語

放下、服務、奉獻

Why do we experience
afflicted mental states?
Because the mind is
fettered by greed, hatred,
delusion, arrogance, and
doubt. This is what needs
to be given up.

人生旅途如同冰雕，
不論好壞都會化成水，
所以一切外相
並不是那麼重要，
只有內心的超越
才是真正要做的事情。

Life is like an ice sculpture: Good or bad, it's bound to melt and disappear. Outer conditions aren't all that important; inner transformation is what really matters.

Seeing the
insubstantiality of both
gain and loss, you can
let go and dwell with a
mind of equanimity.

Selflessness leads to
happiness; constantly
looking out for oneself
generates anxiety.

Joyful Giving:
Letting Go
and Serving Others

喜捨篇
智慧法語

放下、服務、奉獻

Regarding your work
as a way of serving
others brings a sense
of mental poise; this is
the Buddha-dharma.

Joyful Giving:
Letting Go
and Serving Others

喜捨篇

智慧法語

放下、服務、奉獻

When your every thought
is directed towards
benefitting others, others
respond in kind.

退一步替別人想，
大事就會化小事；
如果小不忍就會鬥起來
產生更多不愉快。

Joyful Giving:
Letting Go
and Serving Others

喜捨篇
智慧法語

放下、服務、奉獻

Stepping back and reflecting
on the position of others, a
big deal turns into a trifling
matter. Impatience with
minor problems gives rise to
conflict and regret.

心若能廣大如海，
自然覺得天底下
沒有事情可以干擾到你
縱然有，
也是夢幻泡影；
縱然有，
也是一彈指之間。

Joyful Giving:
Letting Go
and Serving Others

喜捨篇
智慧法語

放下、服務、奉獻

Making your mind
as vast as the ocean,
nothing can disturb
you. And any problem
that does arise doesn't
affect you, for you see
it as nothing more than
a dream, an illusion, a
bubble, or a shadow.

人跟人相處，
常常放不下，
很多的計較就來了。

When we are unable to
let go, our interpersonal
relationships become
fraught with conflict.

不要想向別人討回公道
要能看得破，
心才會平靜，
更不會惹上諸多煩惱。

Joyful Giving:
Letting Go
and Serving Others

喜捨篇
智慧法語

放下、服務、奉獻

If you try to impose
your own lofty
ethical standards on
others, you'll never
be at peace.

和人相處不要有心機，
要直心待人。
直心就是做事一目瞭然
清清爽爽，明明白白。

When you relate to people
in a forthright, transparent
manner, without any hidden
agenda, your interactions
with others will be
smooth and relaxed.

Joyful Giving:
Letting Go
and Serving Others

喜捨篇
智慧法語

放下、服務、奉獻

When you are well established
in the practice, interpersonal
difficulties don't get turned
into major vexations.

Joyful Giving:
Letting Go
and Serving Others

喜捨篇
智慧法語

放下、服務、奉獻

Happiness resides
in giving.

不要整天跟自己過不去
沉溺在人我是非裡
轉不出來。

Don't make life
difficult for yourself by
wallowing in the mire
of competition and
senseless bickering.

當煩惱來時，
要懂得將空的門窗打開

Joyful Giving:
Letting Go
and Serving Others

喜捨篇
智慧法語

放下、服務、奉獻

When afflicted mental states
arise, let them pass out
through the window
of emptiness.

佛法如何破除煩惱？
要常常喜捨布施、
站在別人的立場想。

Buddhism teaches
us how to eliminate
afflicted mental states
by practicing joyful
giving and exchanging
self and other.

常常供養佛、
供養法、供養僧，
供養是非常好的資糧。

Joyful Giving:
Letting Go
and Serving Others

喜捨篇
智慧法語

放下、服務、奉獻

Making offerings to the
Buddha, Dharma, and
Sangha is an excellent
way to lay down
wholesome roots.

日常生活要養成供養、
服務的習慣，廣修供養
就是做最好的服務業。

Joyful Giving:
Letting Go
and Serving Others

喜捨篇
智慧法語

放下、服務、奉獻

Make a habit of
serving others and
making offerings;
this is the best type of
service career.

供養要衡量能力來做，
有多少就供多少，
供養的心才是最重要。

Give according to your
means; it's the
thought that counts.

一顆種子，
可以長出一大串的穗粒。
不要因善小而不為，
小布施一樣有大福報。

A tiny seed can grow
into a great tree. Don't
think that a small gift
is not worth giving.

學習生命、瞭解生命、
珍惜生命，
才能夠奉獻生命。

Only when you
understand and cherish
life will you be able
to make a meaningful
contribution to society.

「慈悲喜捨」的工作，
就是把自己最好的東西
奉獻給別人。

Joyful Giving:
Letting Go
and Serving Others

喜捨篇
智慧法語

放下、服務、奉獻

Really practicing
compassion and joyful
giving, you'll be willing
to give away even
your most cherished
possession.

在生命裡面，
必須時時刻刻
不放棄任何一個
結好緣的機會、
服務的機會、
奉獻的機會。

Joyful Giving:
Letting Go
and Serving Others

喜捨篇

智慧法語

放下、服務、奉獻

Never miss an
opportunity to
connect favorably
with others
through service
and generosity.

福氣就是給人家善緣，
要有善緣
就要改善自己
身、口、意的習氣。

Joyful Giving:
Letting Go
and Serving Others

喜捨篇

智慧法語

放下、服務、奉獻

Good fortune and
wholesome affinities
are the result of
skillful habits in body,
speech, and mind.

如何離開
貪、瞋、癡？
從學習「布施」開始。

Becoming free of greed,
hatred, and delusion all
starts with generosity.

用「不生煩惱便生功德」
的心為人處事，
就會有功德。

Joyful Giving:
Letting Go
and Serving Others

喜捨篇

智慧法語

放下、服務、奉獻

Virtue comes from dealing
with others with a mind
free of defilements.

不要把很多事情
都掛在心頭，
常常要放下，
放得下才是福氣。

Don't let all sorts of
worries clutter your
mind. Continually letting
go brings good fortune.

一切的苦樂
都是因為心的取捨，
才有苦樂；
如果不取捨一切，
就沒有這些苦。

Sorrow is the result
of grasping and
aversion; refraining
from grasping and
aversion leads to the
end of suffering.

「過日子」，
就是什麼東西都讓它過，
不要讓它「不過」——
「過」就可以過日子，
「不過」就不好過日子。

Joyful Giving:
Letting Go
and Serving Others

喜捨篇
智慧法語

放下、服務、奉獻

Allow all things
to come and go
according to their
nature; hanging on to
them is misery.

有人會討厭我們，
要想是自己沒有修行，
所以要常常懺悔、
學習付出，
防止自己的驕慢心。

Joyful Giving:
Letting Go
and Serving Others

喜捨篇
智慧法語

放下、服務、奉獻

If you are disparaged
by others, take it as
an opportunity to
practice self-reflection,
repentance, giving,
and humility.

　　以愛止恨，會感化、
感動對方，彼此都會放下
到最後彼此是一個善緣

Joyful Giving:
Letting Go
and Serving Others

喜捨篇
智慧法語

放下、服務、奉獻

Using love to counter
hatred has a positive effect
on others; it creates the
opportunity for letting go
and ultimately generates
mutual affinity.

Spiritual practice means
dealing with afflicted
mental states as soon as
they arise, without getting
involved with them. Don't
go looking for them; they
will come to you.

Joyful Giving:
Letting Go
and Serving Others

喜捨篇
智慧法語

放下、服務、奉獻

A heart free of
entanglements is as
vast as the ocean.

過去就讓它過去，
未來也不必牽掛，
現在就是把握一個快樂
輕安、慈善、奉獻、
離苦得樂的心，
做好每一件結善緣的工作

Joyful Giving:
Letting Go
and Serving Others

喜捨篇
智慧法語

放下、服務、奉獻

When you stop obsessing
about the past and the future,
the mind spontaneously
becomes tranquil,
benevolent, caring, and
happy—this is a state in
which you easily connect
favorably with others.

佛法是什麼？學佛是從
「拆除大隊」開始做起的

Buddhist practice begins
as a demolition project.

把一切執著障礙都拆了，
你才瞭解佛法；
拆不了世間的假象，
就不懂得佛法。

Joyful Giving:
Letting Go
and Serving Others

喜捨篇
智慧法語

放下、服務、奉獻

Only after demolishing
your attachments,
hindrances, and
illusions can you
really understand the
Buddha-dharma.

我們要解冤解業，
不要把任何恩怨帶到來生
今生就放下，
捨掉這些恩怨。

Let go of all attachment
and resentment whatsoever;
otherwise it will become a
hindrance in your next life.

Joyful Giving:
Letting Go
and Serving Others

喜捨篇

智慧法語

放下、服務、奉獻

To understand birth and
death and be free of
afflicted mental states,
you have to encounter
that which is beyond
birth and death.

Spiritual practice is
all about rectifying
the heart and mind
by letting go of
attachment.

做事要能沒有負擔，
最重要的就是喜捨。

Be in the world, but not
of the world; joyful
giving is the key.

「念佛」讓我們
覺醒很多恩恩怨怨，
能夠放下。

Recollecting the
Buddha, we become
aware of all sorts of
likes and dislikes, and
then let go of them.

Joyful Giving:
Letting Go
and Serving Others

喜捨篇
智慧法語

放下、服務、奉獻

Recollecting the
Dharma, we experience
freedom and stop
generating hindrances.

「念僧」讓我們
清淨安定，不要染濁。

Recollecting the
Sangha, we experience
peace and purity.

學佛，就是要能夠禪修，
從禪修當中
漸漸遠離執著。

Joyful Giving:
Letting Go
and Serving Others

喜捨篇

智慧法語

放下、服務、奉獻

Buddhist practice is
a way of gradually
training the mind to
stop grasping.

最快樂的生命
是知道如何過一個
不執著的生命。

Happiness is a life
free of attachment.

能空一切，便成智慧。

Joyful Giving:
Letting Go
and Serving Others

喜捨篇

智慧法語

放下、服務、奉獻

With an understanding
of emptiness, everything
becomes wisdom.

不要因為虛幻的事情
而起煩惱，一定要有
放下的志氣。

Don't get all bent out
of shape over your
illusory perceptions;
letting go is essential.

對於一切的
好好壞壞、是是非非，
總是安貧守道，
總是無所得的心。

Joyful Giving:
Letting Go
and Serving Others

喜捨篇
智慧法語

放下、服務、奉獻

Regard all things—good
or bad, right or wrong—
with a mind grounded in
contentment and virtue.

心一貪住就會罣礙、
執著、妄想；
不貪住的時候，
心就會回到本來。

Joyful Giving:
Letting Go
and Serving Others

喜捨篇
智慧法語

放下、服務、奉獻

In the wake of craving
come hindrances,
attachment, and
delusion; undisturbed
by craving, the mind
returns to its source.

當我們面臨逆境時，
何不依照佛的智慧去做
在一切處放下。

When we encounter
adversity, we need to
use wisdom to let go.

修行就是一條心路之旅
在心的旅程中
時刻都要無罣無礙、
無念無著，
就可以達到自在禪定。

Joyful Giving:
Letting Go
and Serving Others

喜捨篇
智慧法語

放下、服務、奉獻

Spiritual practice is a
journey of the heart, in
the course of which you
pass beyond attachments
and transcend obstacles
until you reach a state of
complete freedom.

身心就是遇緣自在安定，
不會刻意地去求什麼、
想什麼。

When you are content
in body and mind with
whatever comes up, you
no longer demand that
things go a certain way.

Enlightenment means
coming out of the
fog of confusion.

開悟的人，
處處看破放下；
不開悟的人，處處執著

An enlightened person
sees things clearly and
lets go of them; an
unenlightened person
hangs on at every turn.

眾生總是喜歡在
「有」裡面製造種種煩惱
破除「有」，
進入「空」，
才能解除煩惱。

Our tendency is to
create all sorts of
afflicted mental states
about things we regard
as really existent;
seeing their empty
nature, we become
free of affliction.

空沒有負擔，
提得起、放得下，
失敗成功都可以承擔。

Joyful Giving:
Letting Go
and Serving Others

喜捨篇
智慧法語

放下、服務、奉獻

Relating to life from the
perspective of emptiness,
you can pick things up and
put them down without
being burdened by thoughts
of success or failure.

Joyful Giving:
Letting Go
and Serving Others

喜捨篇 智慧法語

放下、服務、奉獻

Don't cling to any
place or any view.

學習放下煩惱，
讓心在一切處
都沒有蹤跡，
如果處處留蹤跡，
就處處留煩惱。

Joyful Giving:
Letting Go
and Serving Others

喜捨篇
智慧法語

放下、服務、奉獻

Learning how to let
go of defilements,
your mind becomes
trackless; the mind of
defilement leaves a
trace wherever it goes.

因緣變化只是一種組合，
一旦組合的緣盡了，
就會分散。
想要離開煩惱，
就得明白這層道理。

Understanding that
everything arises
and ceases due to
causes and conditions,
afflicted mental states
wane and fall away.

佛法上的造福
就是利他、喜捨的工作，
並不是拚個你死我活、
爭得頭破血流的生活
才是有福氣。

Buddhism teaches that
happiness comes from
benefitting others and
joyful giving, not from
fighting to get to the
top of the heap.

今生會遇到什麼
大部分是註定的，
不要牽強固執，
該來的就來，該去的就去
該有的趕緊珍惜，
不該有的趕緊放掉。

Joyful Giving:
Letting Go
and Serving Others

喜捨篇
智慧法語

放下、服務、奉獻

Our lot in life is
mostly determined in
advance; things come
and go of their own
accord, so cherish
them while they last.

心要在
「有罣礙」裡面放下，
在「有執著」裡面放下。

Learn how to let go in
the midst of impediments
and attachment.

常常訓練這顆心
歸屬於空性，
慢慢地就不會執著，
而生出法喜的快樂。

Joyful Giving:
Letting Go
and Serving Others

喜捨篇
智慧法語

放下、服務、奉獻

By constantly training
the mind to dwell in
emptiness, you slowly
give up clinging and
experience the joy of
the Dharma.

每一個人總是
在自己的感覺裡生活，
這些感覺就是讓我們
嘗受到痛苦的主要原因。

Joyful Giving:
Letting Go
and Serving Others

喜捨篇

智慧法語

放下、服務、奉獻

We live inside
our erroneous
perceptions—this is
the main source
of suffering.

在每一個當下
都能夠把心放鬆，
對事不會貪住執著，
就是解脫，就是放下。

Joyful Giving:
Letting Go
and Serving Others

喜捨篇

智慧法語

放下、服務、奉獻

Relax the mind from
moment to moment
and stop clinging—
this is liberation.

試著從「空」裡面
去安心，也許能夠解決
很多煩惱和困擾，
以及存在於生活上
點點滴滴的壓迫感。

Joyful Giving:
Letting Go
and Serving Others

喜捨篇

智慧法語

放下、服務、奉獻

Allow the mind to
rest in emptiness;
doing so, it
becomes possible to
experience freedom
from anxiety and
mental afflictions.

眾生都是
從「有」上去求，
而佛是從「空」裡
得到解脫。

Joyful Giving:
Letting Go
and Serving Others

喜捨篇
智慧法語

放下、服務、奉獻

Ordinary beings make
demands on what is
erroneously perceived
to really exist; a buddha
attains liberation by
passing through emptiness.

Joyful Giving:
Letting Go
and Serving Others

喜捨篇
智慧法語

放下、服務、奉獻

Vowing to attain
buddhahood, you
experience ease and
freedom at every turn.

福田就是在生活中
服務、奉獻。

Joyful Giving:
Letting Go
and Serving Others

喜捨篇
智慧法語

放下、服務、奉獻

Benefitting others in daily
life is a field of merit.

用清淨心看世間，
世間即清淨；
用解脫的心看世間，
心即解脫。

Joyful Giving:
Letting Go
and Serving Others

喜捨篇

智慧法語

放下、服務、奉獻

Viewing the world with
a pure heart, the world
becomes pure; viewing
the world with the mind
of liberation, the mind
becomes liberated.

布施要以喜悅心去做，
喜悅從無所得來。

Joyful Giving:
Letting Go
and Serving Others

智慧法語

喜捨篇

放下、服務、奉獻

Give with joy in your
heart, without expecting
anything in return.

多一點的奉獻
就是多一點賺到，
少一點的奉獻
就是少一點的福報。

Joyful Giving:
Letting Go
and Serving Others

喜捨篇

智慧法語

放下、服務、奉獻

The more you
give, the more you
gain; giving less,
you shortchange
yourself.

# 心之道 智慧法語（第二輯）

**喜捨篇-放下、服務、奉獻**

心道法師語錄

主　　編：洪淑妍
責任編輯：李慧琳
英文審校：石麗君
美術設計：宋明展
發 行 人：歐陽慕親
出版發行：財團法人靈鷲山般若文教基金會附設出版社
地　　址：23444新北市永和區保生路2號21樓
電　　話：(02)2232-1008
傳　　真：(02)2232-1010
網　　址：www.093books.com.tw
讀者信箱：books@ljm.org.tw
法律顧問：永然聯合法律事務所
印　　刷：皇城廣告印刷事業股份有限公司
初版二刷：2013年8月
定　　價：新台幣180元(1套2冊)
I S B N：978-986-6324-41-3

## The Way of Mind II : Words of wisdom
## Joyful Giving: Letting Go and Serving Others

Words of Dharma Master Hsin Tao
Editor in Chief: Hong, Shu-yan
Editor in Charge: Li, Huei-lin
English Proofreading:Lisa Shih
Art Editor: Song, Ming-zhan
Publisher: Ouyang, Mu-qin
Published by: the Subsidiary Publishing House of the Ling
Jiou Mountain Prajñā Cultural Education Foundation
Address: 21F., No.2, Baosheng Rd., Yonghe Dist., New
Taipei City 23444, Taiwan (R.O.C.)
Tel: (02)2232-1008
Fax: (02)2232-1010
Website: www.093books.com.tw
E-mail: books@ljm.org.tw
Legal Consultant: Y. R. Lee & Partners Attorneys at Law
Printing: Huang Cheng Printing Company, L
The Second Printing of the First Edition: August 2013
List Price: NT$ 180 dollars(Two-Manual Set)
ISBN: 978-986-6324-41-3

# The Way of Mind I

Words of wisdom

**Cultivate Wisdom  Cultivate Mind  Cultivate Spiritualit**

By Dharma Master Hsin Tao

心道法師法語清新如露，滴入人心之力量正如暮鼓晨鐘

讓人在煩惱當下豁然開朗，開啟自性明徹的一方天空

閱讀心道法師語錄，可以讓個人內修自省的功夫

在日常生活中發酵延續，成就自利利他的菩薩行

**修慧篇**

放下執著，
同時也放過自己一馬。
Stop clinging and
give yourself a break!

**修心篇**

心平安，世界就平安了。
When our mind is at peace,
the world is at peace.

**修行篇**

修行，就是找回真實的生命。
Spiritual practice is
just living a life of truth.

隨身智慧寶典

第一輯

心之道

智慧法語　心道法師　語錄

修慧篇／修心篇／修行篇

國家圖書館出版品預行編目(CIP)資料

心之道智慧法語. 第二輯 / 洪淑妍主編. -- 初版.
-- 新北市：靈鷲山般若出版, 2012.12
　 冊 ； 公分
ISBN 978-986-6324-41-3(全套：精裝)

1.佛教說法 2.佛教教化法

225.4                                         101024788